Zoetrope

Hilary Otto

First published 2023 by The Hedgehog Poetry Press

Published in the UK by
The Hedgehog Poetry Press
Coppack House, 5
Churchill Avenue
Clevedon
BS21 6QW

www.hedgehogpress.co.uk

ISBN: 978-1-913499-72-3

9 8 7 6 5 4 3 2 1

A CIP Catalogue record for this book is available from the British Library.

Cover photo by Pedro Lopes on Unsplash

For my parents

Contents

THE ILLUSION OF MOTION

Today, I am animated.
I am a series of horse stills, passing
so fast around a spinning cylinder
that my feet don't touch the ground.
When I gallop, I am jerky-smooth,
I don't tire of this running.
I look like I am moving forward.

I reach back into the dark.
Events flash through my mind
like faces in a zoetrope. Figures
blurred in motion come rushing
out of the slots. People,
animals fling limbs at the air.
They scatter as I approach.

If we draw the right images
in this flip book, we will be capable
of extraordinary things. We'll see
our bodies twist in new shapes
bold in the morning light,
progress spinning ahead of us
but just out of reach –
the memory after the dream.

SCARAB'S GOT TALENT

As I rolled on that stinking ball towards the dawn
the night sky shone its universe on my back,
but my legs buckled. I wanted to be much more than this.
I wanted to be *the one to watch,* to be Betelgeuse!

The night sky shone its universe on my back
with a purpose: to reveal my destination.
I wanted to be *the one to watch,* to be Betelgeuse,
to rise from the dust and start to move again

with a purpose. To reveal my destination,
I dreamt in star trails. I wanted to dance to new tunes,
to rise from the dust and start to move again.
While my lovers slept in their steaming beds,

I dreamt in star trails. I wanted to dance to new tunes,
I needed to find a new route and walk it with grace.
While my lovers slept in their steaming beds,
I was lost and alone on overcast nights.

I needed to find a new route and walk it with grace,
heaving the grubby burden of existence.
I was lost and alone on overcast nights
while a kaleidoscope of ancient light streaked past,

heaving the grubby burden of existence.
When the clouds cleared, I stared in wonder
while a kaleidoscope of ancient light streaked past.
That smudgy galactic stripe drew my path

when the clouds cleared. I stared in wonder
at a clotted vein which bulged across the sky.
That smudgy galactic stripe drew my path
as I rolled on that stinking ball towards the dawn.

A MOTHER'S WORK

I dream of car crashes.
I see kidnaps and shootings,
imagine stabbings in the twilight park
with tents pitched for forensics.

I visualise the empty canoe
bobbing light by the river bank,
and the curl of burning sofas
smoulders through every sleepover.

I picture the pill cut with bleach,
the powder and the overdose.
The fever of *Death by misadventure*
beats a savage rhythm in my temples.

I spread these visions as offerings
to appease the demons that possess me.
In my private A&E a trolley hurtles in,
fills beds with spectres as the doors swing.

PLOT

Here I am in my bloodstained dress
a teenage girl, pale and blonde
emerging from that dark room
where atrocities have taken their time.

Now here I am dying,
staggering towards you, clutching
at nothing in front of me as I fall;
my mouth a lemon slice of despair.

Here you are leaving casually,
stopping to shield a cigarette.
Now here you are taking a shower,
driving to B&Q to buy a shovel.

You might recognise this car interior.
You may feel that you remember
the pattern of the corridor carpet;
the exact sequence of events.

There is a pattern in more things
than the carpet. I repeat myself
dying, always young and bloodstained.
You have been here a million times before.

MANDELBROT

The more we mustn't be,
the more we become.
We repeat, forming
a perfect pattern
retreating
in the heart's eye.
We create complexity
from simplicity.
At our centre
is a hole
and we must
plot relentlessly
on the frayed edge of things.
The more we mustn't be,
the more we become.

HILLS LIKE WHITE ELEPHANTS

One look at the landscape
shows that something is wrong.
In all our views, the same subject:
me, me, me.
Stories about exotic lands
once painted a picture so beguiling
that it became real. A stripping
of detail into a hazy snap
shot with safari helmets.

We understood new places
via the algorithm of our imaginations
we could only describe someone else's hills
in our language.
We became more of ourselves
in more countries. Our heads grew
statues from their bases, settled
on grey plinths and planted
heroic stances on the soil.

We carry these statues on our backs.
We plant them at every crossing, name
our streets for men who made it
into stone.
The hills are in captivity
a zoo animal staring through bars
pacing the dust and tossing its trunk
sweat flecking its back
like vowels.

THE GOLDEN LION

This hunk of Venetian muscle
rippling in gold leaf is a trophy lion.
Plunder adorned with stiff wings.

Blue eyes raised to the heavens,
he prays, grimacing lips painted
scarlet around a protruding tongue.

His tail curves inward, an alien flower
about to strike its own flesh. His mane
falls like a blonde wig, and a rope

of golden hair leads down his belly
to where his cock glints in the light.
He is mostly pious and slightly Vegas.

One forepaw hangs suspended in mid air,
the Gospel long-gone. Imperial might,
reduced to a beckoning Lucky Cat.

Note: A Golden Lion of St Mark statue is displayed in the cellar of the White Tower at the Tower of London. It was looted from the Venetian Fortress in Corfu by British troops in 1809.

TIES

How much power can one thin trimming hold?
This silky charm came from profit and war;
unscrupulous mercenary uniforms
spawned a Louis-scrupulous style of clothes.
And still it drapes itself around the shirts
of power brokers; not for nothing the Windsor
knot, the accidental four-in-hand boater,
belly warmers with secrets on the reverse.
We try to drop it. We open shirts, serve
our Fridays free of starch, we *smart casual*.
But it creeps back, tightens its colonial noose,
binds us to its maleness, plots patriarchy's curve
from battlefield to clapped out business unit,
and begs us, dying, to quick undo it.

THE NATION'S FAVOURITE POEM

you can keep your

lies,

If you can bear to hear the truth

there is nothing
which says

If you

hurt

men

you'll be a Man

UNDERWORLD

We press against the oozing dirt, thrive
on the tang of damp matter. By the time
you become aware of us easing up
from the earth like time-lapse capsules
disturbed, we will have popped out, soiled
as if surprised during private acts, to buff
our bald caps and moisten our pale skin.

Beneath, where you cannot see us work
our spores transform into moons of milk.
Our mycelium threads extend, bind together
and we emerge, fringed with gills to perpetuate
our presence inside those crevices we find
fertile. We look too ordinary to pose a threat.
We are experts at waiting in silence.

WHAT THE DATA ABOUT MIGRATION TOLD ME

We are incoming packets
discrete, carrying our own
context. Our aim is to pass through
without being stored in a session.

We choose the optimal path
for delivery, clustering
at the interface between nodes.
When we encounter a closed path

we redistribute, or use a broker
for dispatch and settlement.
The broker makes decisions
based upon current demand.

If the load is well-balanced
we are outgoing, our movement
is invisible to the receiver
until we reach choke point

we have not yet reached settlement
we are asynchronous threads
                pooling
we are stateless, but we persist

NO SIGNS OF LIFE

we have reached the loading zone where it's harder
to get our bearings, everything glints in sharp sun

the air is piled high with a tetris of containers
blocks of noisy colour against techno blue

we can't see inside but it's people's lives, chicken
in enormous quantities and household goods

i know this because the man from logistics
willingly gave me this information

the way forward is unclear, we wait at a red
overhauled by a double-decker freight train

in its belly caged cars sulk with wheels tethered
jewelled bugs with wings taped shut, headlights blank

we will arrive before they do, but they know more than us
the chickens are dead, the cars can drive themselves

OUTSIDE THE FROZEN ROOM

After Alex Dimitrov

We wade further in
right up to our knees.
Our legs swish through grass
arms swing for momentum
through this relentless air.
There's no edge to this field
it stretches across sage acres
to blend gunmetal sky
with a blurred horizon.
We keep on wading, though
we can't remember why
or exactly where we are headed.
An owl flits past, swoops
on its prey. The field won't
reveal which way it is
facing. Our map is furred
with grass. So soothing, this grass,
that whispers in the breeze
like a soul in flight.
We take time to admire
the view: smooth and featureless
beneath such a wide sky.
Lapwings rise and leave.
We press on. Wherever
we are headed, we'd best
be there before dark.

DINGHY

beside the river, no-one but four schoolgirls
sparks of gorse fringing a shingle beach

we laughed for what seemed like hours just pumping
rubber to plump the boat so it was hard, then off

two rowed, slowly marooning us, the steady splash relaxing
so we laid out despite the gravel brands on our backsides

at once, a man was standing on our slip of shale, we turned
on hearing speaking or did he speak on seeing turning

do you mind if I sit here he said, and sat.
one minute passed then he was wearing nothing but a thong.

in unison in mirrored shades we checked his height, his mass
his weight and lay quite still, not fight nor flight but stiffness

and when we saw he'd gone we didn't speak of him
or where he was but strained to hear the sound of oars

and planned the way to run while carrying a dinghy

A FIELD SEEN FROM THE TRAIN

This shock of violent yellow appears
to come from nowhere each time.
A screaming field; soon out of sight
but still blooming on the memory.

REACTION (1-OCTEN-3-ONE)

they say   blood smells like metal   the air is heavy tonight

     you will not speak about this   on twitter

          there is nothing   like an official statement

we can smell it   like coins sweating in the palm

     your reaction   an absence   touches us

  and we are permanently changed   broken down

we are degraded   feel the transformation   inhale the rage

Note: When hands touch iron, perspiration on the skin adds two electrons to the iron atoms, which then react with skin oils and decompose. This reaction creates the organic molecule 1-octen-3-one, which is responsible for the "metallic" smell that we associate with coins and blood.

HOW SLOW THE SOUND COMES

for a second everything is lit up
but there is no time to register
faces, expressions, to match detail to noise
only the bang, which arrives long after
the hot slap in the chest, in the brain
long after we realise what it brings with it:
shattered glass, people, cars
all vying for space on our vision, impatient
children diving in front of our eyes
which are the only senses working now
it's gone quiet like someone turned on
the mute button because it was all too loud
it is all too loud, and full of dust
as we are made to listen
to what has happened already
to replay what we could not stop
the sound
is all

SMALL ACTS OF REBELLION

to let a train pass without boarding
to stand still on an emptying platform
to allow the rush to flow around you
to amble towards the jammed exit
and pass the barriers humming
to saunter out into the street
to tear your eyes from the light
in your palm and raise them briefly
past the walls looming on all sides
to find the small gap of blue above you
stretching right up to the edge
of the earth's atmosphere
where the particles escape

THE TAIL OF A WHALE

If you are trapped
on a runaway train
that rattles off the tracks
and overshoots the parapet into the open
you may be forgiven
for bracing yourself for impact,
for clamping your jaw tight shut,
for closing your eyes.

As the lights race past the window
you glimpse the city below,
its buildings gathered
in an execution crowd.
The train cuts swiftly through
a featureless night sky
propelled towards the block
of water rippling dark below.

But perhaps today is not your day
to die. You may be surprised
to come to rest with a new angle
hanging suspended above everything
that you thought you knew;
emerging to marvel at the ordinary
wonder of the same world
you stepped off a platform to leave.

You might open the door
to sniff the chill air of the same sky
that had appeared dull minutes before.
You may linger on the tail of a whale
which extends like an afterthought
to ripple the surface of your mind,
and then slide down into the cool waters
of your changed existence.

BLACKBIRD, REMIXED

After RS Thomas, The Beatles, and all the other Blackbirds

Shadows deepen on the grass, privet stalks
the lawn. The day is damping. It's time

                              arise

for me to gather up and go inside.
But one bird reboots the evening,

                                      sweet

and one woman becomes a young girl.
I linger by the indigo hedge and rewind

                         fresh

because of the song that you string
in the air; an old standard remastered

                    rich music

in snatches of ever-more-daring licks.
As you forge new riffs from each refrain

                         passed on

in your jazz solo, you reinvent yourself
in all our spaces. I'm squinting up

                                new

through layers of years retreating into dusk.
The music delivers us past memory and place.

                         orchards

Wherever I am, your song returns
me to the beginning. The soundscape

                    this moment

you create reverberates inside long after
your outline has faded. Shock this darkness

                                      singing

with your brilliance. God knows, we all need
to hear a good tune. Remind us to settle

                     free

on the high points, inspire us to release
our melodies relentlessly against the failing light.

ACKNOWLEDGEMENTS

My thanks to the editors at the following publications where some of the poems in this pamphlet first appeared: *Ink, Sweat & Tears*: "What the data about migration told me"; *The Alchemy Spoon*: "The Nation's Favourite Poem"; *boats against the current*: "small acts of rebellion"; *As It Ought To Be Magazine*: "Underworld"; *Anti-Heroin Chic*: "Mandelbrot"; *The Blue Nib*: "dinghy".

"The Nation's Favourite Poem" uses text from "If" by Rudyard Kipling.

I would particularly like to thank Anna Saunders, John McCullough and Rebecca Goss for their testimonials and general support, and Wendy Pratt for helping to knock my poems into a pamphlet via her excellent course. I'd also like to thank the amazing poetry crew on twitter who have provided constant encouragement and inspiration.

Thanks for everything and love always to Dad, Andrew (AMJSTKA), Simon (SKCE); Victor, Elliot & Dylan; to BFF Zoë for helping with some key decisions; and to the memory of my lovely Mum.

Finally, many thanks to Mark Davidson for choosing my poems and creating such a beautiful book.